WHY MEN OUGHT ALWAYS TO PRAY

BY
ROBERT E. DANIELS

Why Men Ought Always to Pray
ISBN 978-1-936314-25-6
Copyright © 2010 by Robert E. Daniels
P. O. Box 701294
Tulsa, OK 74170-1294

Published by Word & Spirit Books
PO Box 701403
Tulsa, OK 74170
www.wordandspiritresources.com

Project development by PriorityPR Group, Tulsa, Oklahoma

CONTENTS

FOREWORD

I'm honored that God has chosen me to be the vessel by which He would allow the anointing of the Holy Spirit to direct my thoughts, guide my hands, and set my pen in motion in the writing of this book. I have had compassion in my heart for quite some time to minister to the needs of men. While my heart is for both men and women, I have seen where it's been necessary for the man to step up into his position in God first, thereby allowing him to lead his family. When this order is established, we will see a major difference in the family structure, in the Church, and ultimately in the world.

Flowers don't appear in the middle of a solid, frozen winter season but do appear in spring when all conditions are right. I now realize that we can try to make things happen out of season and find that there is no anointing for it. God gave me the material for most of this book a few years ago. It wasn't until a year ago that I made the decision to attempt to pen those thoughts that were rolling around in my head and put them in manuscript form. It did not take me long to realize this would not be as easy as I thought. I knew what I wanted to say, but somehow the words were not flowing on the paper like I had anticipated. It became a chore trying to write the first three paragraphs.

I finally realized that two critical elements seem to be missing. I could not sense the anointing, and the timing seemed to be off. Why was I having so much trouble with the first three paragraphs? It was then that I made the decision to set aside this project for a later time. I asked God to place a desire on my heart and let me know when I was supposed to start this project again. I realized that in order for this book to be written like God wanted it, I had to write it in His timing. I made a vow not to question God about the due season. That is a process that is left totally up to Him. A few months passed and I began to get the desire to pick up the pen and start again. This time I could feel the very presence of God enter my being and the Holy Spirit taking over my hand as I began to pen the manuscript that He had burned in my heart and put it down on paper.

I believe, as Christians, we should do the reasonable services like: live holy, pray daily to God, and follow the directions of the Holy Spirit. Through our obedience, God will surely see to it that due season for all that He has promised comes to pass in our lives.

Glory to God!

SPECIAL ACKNOWLEDGMENT

S pecial acknowledgment goes to Gina Parham for allowing God's anointing to flow through her in helping me to organize my manuscript even in the midst of an already busy time for her. It was also her positive encouragement that helped me stay on course through the completion of the manuscript, even when I wondered whether it would have any impact at all on men's lives.

I knew that I had a strong desire to help effect change in the lives of men, but I wasn't confident enough to believe that this small effort could facilitate any change. She encouraged me to believe that it would.

I would also like to thank Gina's husband, Brent Parham. He is a strong, confident, compassionate "man of God" who displays a strong sense of character. It was his patience and kindness that allowed Gina to dedicate precious time to support my efforts.

I pray that God continues to increase their love for each other, their ministry, and their business in an unparalleled way.

SPECIAL ACKNOWLEDGMENT

My heartfelt thanks goes to my dear friend Vicki, who came along at a time that I call "Ordained by God." This project was pretty much lying dormant. I had been discouraged somewhat about the time it has taken to get the manuscript in print. It has been ready for a few years.

Vicki encouraged me to persist and even set down with me for many hours collaborating together in the final stages of edit preparation.

I'm grateful for her friendship and I thank God for continually blessing her life, the life of her family, and all that she touches.

Thanks Vicki

SPECIAL ACKNOWLEDGMENT

Thank you Anita Dotson for your input into this project. May God richly bless you in all that you do, as I know you have a heart for the "Kingdom of God."

Thanks

DEDICATION

This book can only be dedicated to the Holy Trinity—the Father (God Almighty), the Son (Jesus), and the Holy Spirit (and they are one!). I thank God for creating me. I thank Jesus for shedding His innocent blood for me on the cross. I thank the Holy Spirit for carrying out the thoughts of my heart, channeling the passion of love inside me for God's people, and guiding my hand in the writing of this book.

Amen.

INTRODUCTION

The premise of this book is to show and express to men what God's original plan for man was, and is, through revelation from the Word of God starting with the book of Genesis (the beginning). It is my heartfelt desire that men experience the fullness of life and all that God has to offer. Along with the fullness of life are love, joy, and all of the other fruits of the Spirit.

God's Spirit makes us loving, happy, peaceful, patient, kind, good, faithful, gentle, and self-controlled. There is no law against behaving in any of these ways (Galatians 5:22-23 CEV)

God's fruit shows us His *unconditional* love, so that men can receive a personal revelation through their intimate fellowship time with God like Adam did, recognizing their need to *always pray* to God. We as men need to finally get a revelation in our spirit that it brings great joy to God to know that His sons are prospering in every area of their lives. Men must come to the revelation that God wants them to prosper more than man himself knows or wants to prosper. Let's take a look at 3 John 2 for an illustration of this.

**Beloved, I wish above all things that thou mayest prosper
and be in health, even as thy soul prospereth.**

Man needs to understand that when we start to build anything,
it is necessary to start with a solid foundation. In the beginning
God gave every man that foundation, which is His Holy Word.

If you want to get off to the right start, you must begin with
the Word of God in every endeavor. Prayer is the necessary ingredient that will help you attain success in whatever you put your
mind to. Without prayer you may find that obtaining your goal
may indeed become vain, ineffective, and fruitless at best. *Why
Men Ought Always to Pray* has been written to help you understand that you have unlimited potential in God. Men of God, we
must understand that prayer is a vital and necessary ingredient to
being successful in God.

Through your obedience, God can bring that potential to its
fullness. This brings glory to God, for which He is well pleased.
As one writer has said, "God does not create something for the
purpose of nothing." Therefore at the beginning of your Christian
walk as a born-again believer, you were indwelled with the gift of
the Holy Spirit. Right away, the Holy Spirit had a desire to lead
you forward into all the accomplishments and blessings that God
has designed for your life. After all, the Holy Spirit is a Spirit of
success, accomplishment, progress, and performance, and all the
wonderful and great things of God that lead to completeness and
wholeness. He is available to help you above and beyond your call.

CHAPTER 1:

BUILDING THE RIGHT FOUNDATION

I saiah 28:16 says: "Therefore thus saith the Lord God, behold, I lay in Zion for a foundation a stone, a tried stone, a precious corner stone, a sure foundation: he that believeth shall not make haste." *The Living Bible* says: "A firm, tested, precious cornerstone that is safe to build on." God cannot build on us until we have accepted His Word, settled His Word in our spirit, and made His Word the very fiber of our being—our foundation.

Let's take a moment and talk about the word *foundation.* When people think of the word *foundation,* even when not referring to it in a spiritual sense, most think of something that has been planned and carefully laid out. When I was a boy, I was always fascinated when I passed by construction sites, whether commercial or residential, and saw men standing around appearing to be idling time away watching one or two other men doing the work (finishing experts). It appeared as though these men had no assignment, no direction, or no part in the process. This process usually went on for two to three weeks, and sometimes even longer, depending on the size of the foundation. I didn't really understand that process or what was going on at the time. In later years, I came to realize how tedious a process this was and how delicate the undertaking was. You see, there was a settling process going on. Sometimes it was necessary for the men to just stand around and watch the concrete settle into place before the next stage in the process could begin. Careful planning, excellent timing, patience, and experience were all part of the process. Why? Because they had to make sure that every inch of the foundation was solid. Whether building a two-story house or a fifty-story building, the one thing each structure had in common was their reliability on the stability of the foundation.

The foundation has to be sure, or sound, which explains why it is necessary to have careful planning time. Fifty stories could collapse without the benefit of a sure foundation. Now we are able to see and understand why having a strong foundation is so important. Time itself accelerates the pressures against the foundation. The foundation has to be strong. If you want to build anything successfully, a strong foundation is key. Whether a building is being built or a new relationship is being formed, without a strong foundation the probability for success greatly decreases.

Often, when I write, I like to take the very word itself and look up the meaning of it. Then I am frequently able to gain a deeper interpretation of what it is implying or saying, or the revelation it is bringing. For instance, the word *foundation* can mean "established," "the lowest part of the building," "base," "support," or "endowed institution."

All of these are used to support and give credence to the basic idea for which it stands, that is, support, hold up, assist, and maintain—or we could say "an enriched establishment."

Why wouldn't every child of God want to receive his "enriched establishment" as the center of authority, which is the foundational platform of His Word?

It really goes beyond the platform on which we are first established, but it will serve as a guide for us throughout life.

God wishes that no man (mankind) would perish, but receive His foundational Word for life and be led into His destiny for us, which will ultimately provide the fulfillment in life that we all seek.

There is no limit or height to which we cannot achieve, as God has already made it clear through His Word in Genesis 11 at the Tower of Babel, when these men imagined to build a tower whose top would reach unto heaven: "And the Lord came down to see the city and the tower, which the children of men builded. **And the Lord said, Behold, the people is one, and they have all one language; and this they begin to do: and now nothing will be restrained from them, which they have imagined to do"** (Genesis 11:5-6).

They had no covenant with God, yet the creative imagination that God gave to mankind was active within them. They weren't trying to honor God, but they tapped into a faith principle.

Imagine how much more effective you can be in God's Kingdom once you've cut covenant with Him, allowing Him to be Lord of your life. There is no end; the potential is unlimited, because we are created in God's image. That simply means that as He is a Creator, so are we.

Along with that, as Christians we have an added advantage because we have the power of the Holy Spirit working within us to help us achieve the things we have envisioned, or imagined to do.

The Holy Spirit is on standby, ready, willing, and able to assist us with each endeavor we initiate as it is purposed for us to bring glory to God.

The Holy Spirit is a perfect gentleman, although He will guide us, direct us, and give us the anointing we need to fulfill the vision or purpose, He will not initiate the action. That's why He is known as "helper."

The moment we perceive in our minds that we want to purpose an action that is geared toward glorifying God, the Holy Spirit is on standby, anxiously awaiting our solicitation of His guidance to help fulfill God's plans and purposes here on earth.

For all practical purposes, God created the man to be a vision-ary, and the woman was designed to help him see the plan through.

I would never state that a woman could not have a vision, for many do. From the beginning, however, God designed it such that although man did not have all that he needed alone, God created his helpmeet (the woman) to help the man achieve and fulfill God's plans and purposes here on earth. It was God alone who said, "**It is not good that the man should be alone; I will** make him an help meet for him" (Genesis 2:18). And: "Can two walk together except they be agreed?" (Amos 3:3).

Through further revelation the Holy Spirit has given me, I believe that even that agreement goes beyond the two of them. Man and woman can't look to just each other; they must look to the covenant agreement with God first, which is the only way that they're able to walk together agreed. Agreeing together in God is "A Perfect Love Triangle":

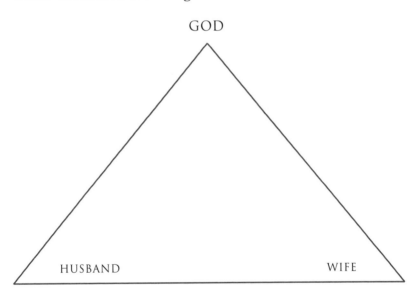

GOD

HUSBAND   WIFE

First Corinthians 3:10 states: "According to the grace of God which is given unto me, as a wise masterbuilder, I have laid the foundation, and another buildeth thereon. But let every man take heed how he buildeth thereupon." The foundation is what God has given to every one of us. It is the basic start in life.

The real process begins with daily prayer, meditation, discipline, a good work ethic, a constant pursuit of excellence, consistency, and most of all, *a developed heart* that is sensitive to the directions of the Holy Spirit.

You will find that by acknowledging God in every step of the process, it becomes a "sweatless" victory, because you are on a path that is directed by God, not merely driven by your own emotions, desires, and efforts. **"In all thy ways acknowledge him and he shall direct thy paths" (Proverbs 3:6).**

Genesis is the foundational chapter or beginning of earth's creation.

"In the beginning God created the heaven and the earth...and the earth was without form, and void; And the Spirit of God moved upon the face of the waters. And God said..."(Genesis 1:1-3). Genesis 1:31 says: "And God saw every thing that he had made, and, behold, it was very good. And the evening and the morning were the sixth day."

God's spoken word brought everything into existence that He said and declared. Nothing basically comes to pass in your life without speaking or declaring the Word of God over it, except by the grace of God. **Genesis 1:2-3 says: "The earth was barren, with no form of life; it was under a roaring ocean covered with darkness. But the Spirit of God was moving over the water. God said, 'I command light to shine!' And light started shining"** (CEV). And we know through our scripture reading that everything *God said* came into existence: **"So shall my word be that goeth forth** out of my mouth: it shall not return unto me void, but it shall accomplish that which I please, and it shall prosper in the thing whereto I sent it" (Isaiah 55:11).

Let's take a look at how powerful the spoken Word of God is.

- **Genesis 1:3: And God said,** Let there be light: and there was light.

- **Genesis 1:6: And God said,** Let there be a firmament in the midst of the waters, and let it divide the waters from the waters.

- **Genesis 1:9: And God said,** Let the waters under the heaven be gathered together unto one place, and let the dry land appear: and it was so.

- **Genesis 1:11: And God said,** Let the earth bring forth grass, the herb yielding seed, and the fruit tree yielding fruit after his kind, whose seed is in itself, upon the earth: and it was so.

- **Genesis 1:14–15: And God said,** Let there be lights in the firmament of the heaven to divide the day from the night; and let them be for signs, and for seasons, and for days, and years: And let them be for lights in the firmament of the heaven to give light upon the earth: and it was so.

- **Genesis 1:24: And God said,** Let the earth bring forth the living creature after his kind, cattle, and creeping thing, and beast of the earth after his kind: and it was so.

- **Genesis 1:26–28: And God said,** Let us make man in our image, after our likeness: and let them have dominion over the fish of the sea, and over the fowl of the air, and over the cattle, and over all the earth, and over every creeping thing that creepeth upon the earth. So God created man in His own image, in the image of God created he him; male and female created He them. And God blessed them, **and God said** unto them, Be fruitful, and multiply, and replenish the earth, and subdue it: and have dominion over the fish of the sea, and over the fowl of the air, and over every living thing that moveth upon the earth.

- **Genesis 1:29: And God said,** Behold, I have given you every herb bearing seed, which is upon the face of all the earth, and every tree, in the which is the fruit of a tree yielding seed; to you it shall be for meat.

If the words that are spoken can actually come into being, as God just proved to us in His Word, shouldn't we be concerned about what we say? Have you ever heard the saying, "You have what you say"? Men of God, what are you saying about your foundation? Is your foundation strong or weak? Let me give you an example of someone who may be building a weak foundation. The words they speak could sound like this.

"I can barely make ends meet. I am about to lose all that I have worked so hard for. I may get fired from my job, and then what am I going to do? If I lose my job, my wife may leave me. Things are so bad I just want to die. I need to work three jobs in order to make it. I am a terrible husband and father. God does not even hear my prayers. I don't believe in God. The Bible is just a history book. There is no way out for me. I hate my life. I have made so many mistakes I don't see how I can

recover. I've been in prison for the last ten years; I don't even know how to live in society anymore. I'm not taking care of my son. I did not tell her to have my baby. She's got some nerve to take child support out on me. All I wanted from her was 'pleasure for a moment'. I need just one more drink to calm my nerves. I have lost all of my inhibitions. I want a divorce. I need a younger woman. All my problems would be solved if I just had more money."

A person talking like this will find themselves on a foundation built in quicksand sinking fast. The devil loves this type of person and will do everything within his power to make sure that what was spoken will surely come to pass. If you are this person, the time has come for you to change the way you talk. Your negative self-talk is slowly but surely destroying you. My brother, you need to change the way you talk and start rebuilding a stronger foundation.

Don't live another day on a weak foundation built on quicksand. God has given you the ability to build a strong foundation with His help and guidance. God's love for you is unconditional, in spite of any past mistakes or failures. He doesn't even hold you to past sins when you repent. His method of operation is to restore and continue; He is the God of progression. Let's take a look at someone who is building a strong foundation.

"God, I am having a challenge paying all of my bills on time or ahead of time. Give me wisdom and show me how to increase my finances and provide for my family properly. I am not in fear of losing my job because I know that God is my source. If this job is over, then all that means is that God has another job waiting for me. I thank You,

Father, for showing me where my new job with a nice increase is. By faith God has given me a Proverbs 31 woman. I shall have what I say. She is bone of my bone and flesh of my flesh. She loves and honors me because I love her. She will not leave me or forsake me because I'm going through a challenging time. The devil is a liar. She understands that this is only a season and we will pass through this 'Valley of the Shadow of Death' in victory. We will continue to serve God and pay our tithes even in the midst of trouble. I'm not moved by what I see. I walk by faith and not by sight. Things cannot get bad enough for me to want to die. I have too much to live for. God has a plan for my life, and I intend to complete the task with the 'Spirit of Excellence'. God did not create me to work three jobs; I'd never have time for my family or God, for that matter. I will pray and ask God for wisdom to provide me with the right job to make the income I need to support me and my family. I am the head of my household and the priest. I am the one who is responsible for my family living for God. I would be a fool not to believe in God. I know that He hears my prayers because I read it in the Word. As 1 John 5:14 states: 'And this is the confidence that we have in him, that, if we ask any thing according to his will, he heareth us: And if we know that he hears us, whatsoever we ask, we know that we have the petitions that we desired of him.' I know that the Bible is more than a history book. It is 'life and health' to all those who believe and speak it by faith: 'For they are life unto those that find them, and health to all their flesh' (Proverbs 4:22). There is a way out for me. God knows better than I do. I'll just continue to pray and believe that God will provide the answers that I need. I will recover from all my mistakes. God has not given me the spirit of fear

but of power, love, and a sound mind. I can do all things through Christ which strengthens me. I am the head and not the tail. I will take care of all of my kids. I helped create them and I will provide for them even if their mother and I don't marry. I will still be in my child's life and I will make a difference. I don't need another drink to solve my problem or make the pain go away. The Holy Spirit can charge me spiritually without the depression that comes with alcohol. When I develop my relationship with God, He will show me the way out. I'm not going to destroy my wonderful marriage by committing adultery with a Jezebel. Proverbs tells me that she makes her bed in hell and will end up taking me there with her as I lie in her bed. I'm tempted but I've got enough God sense to say 'No!' to the temptation. I have too much to lose for a moment's pleasure. I'm not leaving the woman I have built my life with for a younger woman. I can't afford the repercussions of such a disastrous decision. How could I make a covenant with my wife before God, family, and friends and then leave because I found a younger version of my wife? That's something a fool would do. I will be faithful to my wife with the help of God, Jesus, and the Holy Spirit to guide me."

This type of person is well on their way to fulfilling God's plan for their life. When storms or difficult times come, this foundation will be able to stand the assault because God is at the center. Problems will arise, but the destroyer will find it extremely difficult to destroy this foundation. If you are talking like this, you are well on your way to living a totally victorious life.

If you are talking like the person who has a weak foundation, it is not too late to change. Start by changing the way you speak.

You have several examples with which to start. Try saying some positive things over yourself. Stop saying what you think you cannot do. Start saying, "I can do all things through Christ who strengthens me." You have spoken enough negative things over yourself. Don't you think it is time to start saying something positive? Go home and thank your wife for marrying you. Tell your fiancée that you will be a God-fearing man and will provide for her always. Tell your kids that as for you and your house, you will all be serving the Lord. Set the example for your family, friends, and coworkers to follow. You can do it. I have faith in you. To God be the glory!

CHAPTER 2:

THE ANOINTING OF THE HELPMEET

After the foundation was established, which is the Word of God, God, with His infinite wisdom, saw a need in man's life, an anointed helpmeet. With all that God had personally done for the man (Adam) through His own personal touch, I find it interesting that He could recognize a further need. You see, the Bible says: **"And the LORD God formed man of the dust of the ground, and breathed into his nostrils the breath of life; and man became a living soul"** (Genesis 2:7). God didn't form the woman the same way. She was already inside of the man once God had formed him. She was taken out of the man. I believe that was in order for completion. Whatever was taken out, had to be put back in. Therefore, the institution of marriage was ordained by God so that the man would receive his missing part in holy matrimony, creating one whole person in the husband and wife as one flesh. Glory to God! That's why men of God should not be in denial of the fact that they need anointed help: **"This was the Lord's doing, and it is marvellous in our eyes"** (Mark 12:11).

"A virtuous woman is a crown to her husband" (Proverbs 12:4). When you look at a king and see him with his long robe, rings on his fingers, chains of gold around his neck, and all sorts of jewels about him, it may bring him recognition of material wealth or possessions, yet without the anointed crown upon his head, the greatest symbol of kingship is missing. The crown is symbolic of the finishing touch. A man can be anointed in many areas of his life, yet find a need (which he may not always be aware of) for help in channeling those anointings in the right direction as to bring the greatest glory to God. I've known men who have achieved great success in life, and in most instances, were blessed with virtuous wives who fit right into the role of "finishing touch." Men who are secure in God should never suffer difficulties in acknowledging that help, nor giving thanks for it.

- Proverbs 18:22: "Whoso findeth a wife findeth a good thing, and obtaineth favour of the LORD."
- Proverbs 31:10: "For her price is far above rubies."
- Proverbs 31:11: "The heart of her husband doth safely trust in her."
- Proverbs 31:12: "She will do him good and not evil all the days of her life."
- Proverbs 31:26: "She openeth her mouth with wisdom; and in her tongue is the law of kindness."
- Proverbs 31:28: "Her children arise up, and call her blessed; her husband also, and he praiseth her."

Glory to God!

Therefore, brethren, you may safely conclude that finding the virtuous wife that God has for you will satisfy three basic areas. First, it will please you; second, God will be pleased; third, God will acknowledge His pleasure by showing you favor. With the anointed help in your life, you are able to close one chapter in your life. That particular search is over. Together, you're able to create new chapters in your lives. You are now able to dedicate your lives to God for ministry purposes, in whatever way God has ordained it. Amen! Glory goes to God.

THE PROCESS

To understand the process you will need to follow to get there, you must take into consideration **Genesis 2:21-22: "And the LORD God caused a deep sleep to fall upon Adam, and he slept: and he took one of his ribs, and closed up the flesh instead thereof: And the rib, which the LORD God had taken from man, made he a woman, and brought her unto the man."** God brought the best unto Adam. Maybe if Adam had been in on the process of making the woman, he would have been suggesting to God what he needed in a companion. But God already knew his needs. **"For your heavenly Father knoweth that ye have need of all these things" (Matthew 6:32).**

There are many things you need to know about the nurturing process. In Genesis 2:18, because God recognized the need for Adam to have a helpmeet in his life, He brought her forth with certain anointings. That's why you must allow the freedom of expression of that help. One of the gifts that God created in Eve was the gift of instinct, or discernment. That is, she would recognize Adam's needs as they arose. An anointed helper cannot help unless you allow them to. Your confidence comes from prayer to God. Men ought always to pray.

The process that worked for Adam is actually the best process to getting a mate. It's painless. Adam didn't have to do any of the work himself—that is, searching around, looking, wondering, hoping, or any other time-consuming process. There was no emotional stress, no heartache, no disappointment, and no setbacks, as many have experienced in their pursuit of that perfect, mature helpmeet. For all I know, Adam could have just been lying there asleep, smiling and dreaming sweet dreams of what God was manifesting in his life. As much love as God had for Adam, he needed the Ephesians 3:20 blessing, which was exceeding abundantly above all that he could ask or think, according to the power that was working in him. And what was working in him was the anointed power of the Holy Spirit.

I had to be honest with God. I told Him that the reason I never really asked Him to bring me a helpmeet is that I didn't trust what He would bring me, or I didn't know if I would like what He would bring me. I called it being honest with God, but God already knows our every thought. It is good sometimes to just open up and level with God concerning your thoughts and imaginations. He won't condemn you for it. It allows for a greater level of intimacy with Him. I'm reminded of **Matthew 7:9-11,** when Jesus was speaking: **"Or what man is there of you, whom if** his son ask bread, will he give him a stone? Or if he ask a fish, will he give him a serpent? If ye then, being evil, know how to give good gifts unto your children, how much more shall your Father which is in heaven give good things to them that ask him?"

I have heard many believers say, "Oh, you'd better make sure you give God all the details, and name every single thing you want in your mate." To an extent, it may be partially okay, but even greater, no one can convince me that the loving Father God Almighty, whom I serve, is going to give His children stones instead of bread. If you're going to pray for specifics, don't get in bondage after you pray, thinking that because you left off one small detail that God is now going to deliver to you something burdensome, unwanted, or unappreciated. Before you allow yourself to get in any such bondage (which hinders your prayers), pray! Pray, "Lord, I've put my petition before You in prayer, and although I may have left off some necessary details in my request, I plead **Ephesians 3:20**, which says, '**Now unto him that is able to do exceeding abundantly above all that we ask or think, according to the power that worketh in us.**' Lord, my personal experience with You is that You are a good God, the only true and living God. I put you in remembrance of Your Holy Word in **Isaiah 43:26**: '**Put me in remembrance: let us plead together: declare thou, that thou mayest be justified.**' Now Father, I declare in the name of Jesus, that I will receive exceeding abundantly above all that I have asked with regard to my prayer for my helpmeet. Glory to God!" Now, you're out from under any bondage or potential bondage, and your prayer is not hindered for lack of confidence.

"**Beloved, if our heart condemn us not, then have we confidence toward God" (1 John 3:21).** Believe in your heart and let the Lord know that you are confident that He will bring what you have prayed to pass. Recognize that that due season is up to Him. Now, having said all of that, and because **Proverbs 18:22** says: **"Whoso findeth a wife findeth a good thing, and obtaineth favour of the LORD,"** don't be in bondage about your choice. It mostly depends on where your level of confidence is at present. If you feel that you want to search or look for a wife, it's okay, otherwise, God would not have said, **"Whoso findeth a wife findeth a good thing" (Proverbs 18:22).** That's why "men ought always to pray."

"**In all thy ways acknowledge him, and he shall direct thy paths" (Proverbs 3:6).** The paths He directs you on are the right paths. You can also be certain that He allows for the right potentials to cross that path. The selection process is up to you.

CHAPTER 3:

NOT BECOMING DISILLUSIONED IN MARRIAGE

I've heard married men and women alike confess how much time they could devote to God if they did not have spouses. Not that my devotion to God is necessarily any greater than theirs (though I do spend quality time talking to God quite often), it doesn't benefit *God* when you spend time with Him. It benefits *you*. There are many times when I reflect on thoughts of how my anointed marriage will be and the benefits of having a virtuous wife in my life. Now that doesn't mean that when I marry, the time I once spent thinking of marriage will now be devoted to God. It would sound so holy to say, "Oh yes, yes, yes, yes. Amen!" But it isn't a commitment that I know that I will keep. I would rather just ask God to help me organize my time so that I will make the best use of it when it comes to devoting that time to Him. I want to ask *Him* how I could best serve or minister to the needs of His people as He would have me to. Then, I'd thank Him for that guidance. Amen!

If you're already married, don't speculate about how you would devote more time to God if you were not married. The fact remains that you are married, and there are only two ways out of it. First, you and your spouse would have to be separated by death, or second, you would be separated by divorce through the court system. I won't even elaborate on divorce by the courts, because it's a decision that two people usually make based on their own justification, leaving God out of the process.

Often couples speculate about how they could be more devoted to God if they didn't have a spouse. These emotions derive from marriages taken for granted by one or both parties where once joy, satisfaction, and perhaps a sense of purpose was found. But when the marriage doesn't seem to be quite so fulfilling, people want to look to other avenues for the missing elements. You may have once been diligent in the pursuit of marriage at the beginning, because you believed you would be completed as a man in the relationship (and the same is true for a woman). But if you believe that Jesus is the Author, then you must also allow Him to be the Finisher of your faith in every area.

Marriage is a wonderful institution because God ordained it. I believe that it's the second greatest covenant that we can experience. Our covenant relationship with God will always be first. That's why God did not make marriage the life-sustaining force; it is meant to augment our lives so as to bring greater success to us as individuals. The individual need for God *alone* is the sustaining force in life. Marriage should never be taken for granted. There is power in this union when God is allowed in on every phase of it. I'm reminded of **Ecclesiastes 4:9, 10**, and **12**: "**Two are better than one; because they have a good reward for their labour. For if they** fall, the one will lift up his fellow: but woe to him that is alone when he falleth; for he hath not another to help him up. And if one prevail against him, two shall withstand him; and a threefold cord is not quickly broken." I believe that *Jesus* is the third part of that cord. I believe that when the husband and wife come together in covenant and allow Jesus to be intertwined and interwoven into their marriage as the threefold cord, it allows for greater cohesiveness in that marriage. When the storms come, the marriage will not lose its bond. Glory to God!

When I was a young boy growing up in the country, I would often (along with other boys) pull down the long switch-like branches hanging from the willow trees in the summer and make whips out of them. We would always plait them in threes, similar to the plaiting of a little girl's hair. When we tried to twirl them around in twos, they always came apart. But when we included the third branch, they bonded and produced greater cohesiveness and strength. Even a little girl's hair stays together better with three strands braided together as opposed to two.

If you are in a marriage and feel as though you have been misdirected and set off course, or if you feel as though you are stagnant or have lost your zeal for your marriage, I strongly suggest you get before God and rededicate your marriage to Him. I believe that God will immediately set your marriage back on course. I know that God would be more than pleased to add His anointing to a marriage that has grown lukewarm.

Married couples (who *should be* putting tens of thousands to flight) first need to understand the principle of being faithful over that which is least. That would put you in a position to be faithful over much. One of the biggest deceptions that satan has put over the Church is division and strife. People do not realize that the fight is not with each other, but against spiritual wickedness exalting itself against them. Understand that you have to perfect your relationship in this lesser covenant of marriage in order to perfect your relationship with God.

Don't come to God and expect to have a perfect relationship with Him when you're constantly sowing seeds of discord at home. **"Can two walk together, except they be agreed?" (Amos 3:3).** Ask yourself that question.

If you are married, renew yourself in the Word of God and make a commitment to live marriage God's way. You will start to see the fruit of your labor right away. God will cause supernatural things to happen in your relationship because of His pleasure at seeing you include Him in everything concerning your marriage.

Ephesians 5:22-33 says: **"Wives, submit yourselves unto your own husbands, as unto the Lord. For the husband is the head of the wife, even as Christ is the head of the church: and he is saviour of the body. Therefore as the church is subject unto Christ, so let the wives be to their own husbands in every thing. Husbands, love your wives, even as Christ also loved the church, and gave himself for it; that he might sanctify and cleanse it with the washing of water by the word, that he might present it to himself a glorious church, not having spot, or wrinkle, or any such thing; but that it should be holy and without blemish. So ought men to love their wives as their own bodies. He that loveth** his wife loveth himself. For no man ever yet hated his own flesh; but nourisheth and cherisheth it, even as the Lord the church: for we are members of his body, of his flesh, and of his bones. For this cause shall a man leave his father and mother, and shall be joined unto his wife, and they two shall be one flesh. This is a great mystery: but I speak concerning Christ and the church. Nevertheless let every one of you in particular so love his wife even as himself; and the wife see that she reverence her husband."

It is a good practice for you to go back to these verses, recite them with your spouse, and ask God to give you a greater revelation of them in your spirit. That will allow you to see the importance of them for maintaining fulfilled marriages. Remember in verse 32 it says: "**This is a great mystery: but I speak concerning Christ** (the anointing) **and the church.**" The word *mystery* in itself means "above human intelligence." That's why God says that He speaks concerning Christ (the anointing). It wasn't intended that you comprehend it with your human intelligence or reasoning. You need the anointing of Christ to get the revelation. God is more than able and willing to give it to all who ask. That's why it may often be frustrating and difficult to carry out. God is not asking you to figure out this mystery. Just ask the Holy Spirit for direction.

As a married man, you have a great responsibility when it comes to marriage, you should welcome that responsibility. Therefore, take the initiative and just love your wife, even as Christ also loved the Church and gave Himself for it. Make a commitment to do so, and then do it. It would make for a glorious

Church, and that's what Jesus is coming back for. We would be rid of the spots and wrinkles. Do your part to stop the field day that satan's been having in the Body of Christ through deceptive works and practices in holy marriages.

My prayer for every married man of God is that you each get a revelation from God in your spirit, of the need to always appeal to the little girl inside your wife. The little girl who was once in her, still is there. She needs nurturing, loving acts of kindness expressed toward her, and continuous reassurance that she can trust in you and that you'll always have her best interest at heart. Once you allow yourself to appeal to the little girl in your wife, you will respond to her as a loving father would toward his little girl. I haven't known a loving father to act selfishly, uncaring, resentful, or jealous. A loving father does not express distasteful, harsh words toward his little girl. Because he sees her as his little princess, he wishes for her to have all the best that life has to offer. He will even sacrifice of himself to help her achieve that level of accomplishment for her life. When she's happy, he rejoices because it's a part of himself that is being fulfilled. For a man to achieve this level of security, ask for direction from the Holy Spirit. Ask the Holy Spirit to be a conscious reminder to you to always express unconditional love toward your wife, even when your emotions don't seem to want you to do so. *The Holy Spirit can take you places that your emotions won't.*

You can, and will, liberate your marriage through the direction of the Holy Spirit. Remember **Philippians 4:13: "I can do all things through Christ which strengtheneth me."** Amen.

CHAPTER 4:

GIFTS AND CALLINGS IN LIFE

K eeper of the garden, fisher of men, pastor, teacher, evangelist…whatever your calling is in life, God has a special anointing for it. God had a special plan for Adam's life. He wanted Adam to have only the knowledge of good. Adam's intimate times of fellowship with God were of a very special nature. Adam confided in God in every way he knew possible. I believe God cherished those times. After all, God created man in His image and likeness. How could God not like Himself?

Adam's work started with the best that God had to offer. God delighted in His creation. God started Adam off as chief executive officer (CEO). Adam worked his way down to manual labor due to disobedience, as disobedience has consequences. When God brought His special gift (Eve) to Adam, it was intended to be just that—a gift. You should always be able to make the distinction between the gift and the giver. God wanted the gift to help augment Adam's life, not redirect it. That's why you must never worship the gift, but worship the giver only—God.

Isn't it interesting that after Adam's fall from grace, how God reworked the whole institution of man's attainment of ultimate success. Greatness was bestowed upon Adam (the CEO) without his having to work his way up through the ranks.

I think it was merely out of Adam's pure love and fellowship with God. God adored him and he adored God. Yet, after he went astray, or away from God's ordinances, God set a new institution in place.

After Adam's sin in the garden, God handed down His mandate (punishment) upon man. **Genesis 3:17 reads: "And unto Adam he said, Because thou hast hearkened unto the voice of thy wife, and hast eaten of the tree of which I commanded thee, saying, thou shalt not eat of it: cursed is the ground for thy sake; in sorrow shalt thou eat of it all the days of thy life; thorns also and thistles shall it bring forth to thee; and thou shalt eat the herb of the field; in the sweat of thy face shalt thou eat bread, till thou return unto the ground; for out of it wast thou taken: for dust thou art, and unto dust shalt thou return."**

I believe God was saying, if you want to get to the top again, it will be by constantly glorifying God in your life, through praying to God, following the lead of God's "Holy Spirit," adhering to His Word, relying on His Word, understanding that man's goings are of the Lord, and being convinced in your mind that there is no other way.

That way, you won't take for granted your position once it is attained. You now have a revelation in your spirit about what it took to get there. Your focus is now back on God. No other voice outside of His will you hearken to. You'll get the revelation of what it is to achieve from one level of glory to the next. You haven't had it all thrust upon you. You'll guard it with prayer, and you'll keep it with constant thanksgiving. You'll be mindful of the sacrifices it took to get there. You'll glorify God in the highest. You won't allow intruders to invade your territory or penetrate your covenant space. And though it may seem a bit harsh compared to what you were accustomed to from the beginning, you'll come to understand that it is based on His unconditional love for you. It will benefit you. He is still your heavenly Father. Jesus came that you might have life, and life more abundantly.

When you rob God of intimate fellowship and devote that time to other things, you become less sensitive to the voice of God when He is calling. I believe God wanted to direct Adam in every way, even after Eve succumbed to the temptations and wiles of the devil through his deception. Eve fell victim to satan by settling herself under his authority. Adam was not deceived, but his compromised decision to yield to Eve's persuasion put him under the same authority that she was under, that of satan. It established an out-of-order relationship, with Eve heading, Adam following. At that point Adam's sensitivity to the voice of God had been greatly impaired.

Intimate fellowship time with God sharpens your spiritual senses. In the face of temptation, God speaks to your spirit and warns you of things to come. God gave Adam instructions, but Adam had become dull of hearing as a result of his decision (his own self-will). Without relying on the direction of God, Adam fell from grace. You always need to hear God's instructions. "Men ought always to pray."

When God gives you gifts, enjoy the gifts but exalt the giver—God. He will continue to bless you with immeasurable gifts, on and on. He just needs to know that you have clearly made the distinction. God the giver should be worshiped, praised, and exalted. What God gives should be enjoyed, taken care of, cherished, nourished, showed appreciation for, loved, and given thanks for. Although disobedience has consequences, we can all be made righteous through the gift of the Holy Spirit. We can be put in right standing with God when we make Him Lord and Savior of our lives.

Like me, I'm sure you've been disobedient, or have not moved forward in some good opportunity that God has given you, yet, through your repentance of sins and failures, God will keep you on the right path. Glory to God! There is a place in God where He allows for His perfect will to be established in your life. His perfect will is revealed when you keep a daily, intimate relationship with Him, laying aside your self-will and being perfected by God.

I believe Adam's failure came as a result of his continued decrease of intimate fellowship with God. His hearing became dull. How can you be directed if you can't hear God's instructions? You must make a constant effort to stay before God in prayer. He knows the way, because He is the Way. **"Man's goings**

are of the LORD; how can a man then understand his own way?"
(Proverbs 20:24).

In general, we all want to know our destiny in life, and we all
desire to follow on the path that is going to lead us to success in
life. There is basically no difference in what the people of God
want and what the people of the world want as far as success
goes. Financial stability, loving family relationships, and a sense of
purpose is what one would probably call success. However, there
is only one way to achieve all these things without the devastation
and disparity that is so often seen in the world. That way is God's
way. True joy comes from a man's spirit being at peace in the
inner man. Only God can fulfill that desire.

CHAPTER 5:

GOD'S GIFT IN YOU WILL BE MANIFESTED TO ALL

"**N**eglect not the gift that is in thee, which was given thee by prophecy, with the laying on of the hands of the presbytery. Meditate upon these things; give thyself wholly to them; that thy profiting may appear to all" (1 Timothy 4:14-15). Once the basic foundation is laid and you have received gifts and callings from God, there is a specific work that God has ordained for you. You needn't concern yourself whether or not you are too early or too late. You are indeed right on time, and on schedule. "**To everything there is a season, and a time to every purpose under the heaven**" (Ecclesiastes 3:1). Glory to God!

I wondered at times whether I had missed my calling, shown up too late for it, or if it had just passed me by. However, there were several things to remember. First, Jesus had thirty years of anointed preparation time before engaging in three and a half years of anointed preaching, teaching, and healing. Also, God is not in the habit of wasting gifts that He has given to His children. After feeding the five thousand, Jesus said: "**Gather up the fragments so that none are wasted**" (see John 6:12). Romans

11:29 states: "For the gifts and calling of God are without repentance." In other words, His gifts and callings are "irrevocable." Make a choice to take the Word of God over your circumstances, over what it appears to be, or over what people may think or say. And, according to **Philippians 1:6: "Being confident of this very thing, that he which hath begun a good work in you, will perform it until the day of Jesus Christ."**

So, if you've had any confusion along these lines, quickly remove any doubt or unbelief. If God is for you , who can be against you? **"What shall we then say to these things? If God be for us, who can be against us?"** (Romans 8:31). Also, Ecclesiastes 9:7, 10 says: **"For God now accepteth thy works. Whatsoever thy hand findeth to do, do it with thy might; for there is no work, nor device, nor knowledge, nor wisdom, in the grave, whither thou goest."** Whatever your hands find to do, do it to the best of your ability and put all of your strength into it. Do it like it is the most important thing to you. There is no knowledge or wisdom in the grave, so do it while you have an opportunity in your physical body. **Verse 11 reads: "I returned, and saw under the sun, that the race is not to the swift, nor the battle to the strong, neither yet bread to the wise, nor yet riches to men of understanding, nor yet favor to men of skill; but time and chance happeneth to them all."**

Yes, there are men whom you'll find in the race with gifts of swiftness, some possess great wisdom and understanding, and others are great men of skill, but time and chance happened to them all, every one of them. Get busy in the work of God, put your hands to the plow, and consistently do what you have to do.

Then, the time (the due season) and the chance (the opportunity) will happen to you just like it happened to them. But you must be about the Father's business. God did not reward them because of their great individual talents, but because He promised to reward the work of your hands. God would rather take someone who is not so gifted, talented, or wise, and anoint them to do His work. That way, they should only glorify God for a mighty work.

God looks more at your willingness of heart than your ability alone. So remember God's Word in **1 Corinthians 1:26-29: "For ye see your calling, brethren, how that not many wise men after the flesh, not many mighty, not many noble, are called: but God hath chosen the foolish things of the world to confound the wise; and God hath chosen the weak things of the world to confound the things which are mighty; and base things of the world, and things which are despised, hath God chosen, yea, and things which are not, to bring to nought things that are: that no flesh should glory in his presence."** Glory to God!

Also, when it comes to your calling, or due season, be reminded that Jesus spent thirty years of anointed preparation time before three and a half years of anointed healing and teaching. Those thirty years included daily prayer to the heavenly Father for directions. Those thirty years also included great sacrifice and an obedient spirit to the Father, as well as doing the will of the Father only. Jesus said in **John 8:29: "I do always those things that please the Father."**

At this point, it is important to make open declarations before God, and there is no better way than to speak God's own words back to Him. Hebrews 13:20-21 says: "Now the God of peace, that brought again from the dead our Lord Jesus, that great shepherd of the sheep, through the blood of the everlasting covenant, make you perfect in every good work to do his will, working in you that which is wellpleasing in his sight, through Jesus Christ, to whom be glory for ever and ever. Amen."

In line with the task that God has called you to, narrow down the choices to perhaps only a few things, and then select in order the things that come natural for you or the things that you seem to do effortlessly. Chances are, there's a greater anointing to do those things than there is to do the other things. God will give you a greater anointing for the things you genuinely like to do as opposed to the things you find difficult or burdensome. God likes seeing you find great pleasure and joy in the things you do for Him.

Finally, when you have selected that particular endeavor, give yourself wholly to it. Perform it with diligence and faithfulness, and you will see a tremendous increase in God's anointing over your life. By being faithful in this area, God will spread the anointing to other areas of your life. Amen!

Confess the Word of God from Psalm 138:8: "The LORD will perfect that which concerneth me: thy mercy, O LORD, endureth for ever: forsake not the works of thine own hands."

CHAPTER 6:

STUDY GOD'S WORD TO SHOW YOURSELF APPROVED UNTO HIM

Once you have identified the particular task or tasks that you are to do for God and begin to walk in the fullness of that anointing, perform it to the best of your ability. You must look to the Word day and night, allowing the Holy Spirit to perform through you above and beyond your natural ability. **"This book of the law shall not depart out of thy mouth; but thou shalt meditate therein day and night, that thou mayest observe to do according to all that is written therein: for then thou shalt make thy way prosperous, and then thou shalt have good success"** (Joshua 1:8).

Challenges will come while doing ministry work. Don't be naïve to believe that the enemy sits idly by, applauding your efforts on behalf of the things that you're doing for God. The enemy's mission is to steal, kill, and destroy (John 10:10). But the good news is that He that is in us is greater than he that is in the world (1 John 4:4). While the evil one will try to challenge your mission from God, remember **Luke 10:19: "Behold, I give unto** you power to tread on serpents and scorpions, and over all the power of the enemy: and nothing shall by any means hurt you."

When we study the Word of God, He gives us answers to things that we have been searching for, plus we get revelation through His Word through the direction of the Holy Spirit. Read the book of Joshua. In chapter one, Joshua was commanded by God to take the reins from Moses to lead the children of Israel across the Jordan River. God had, in fact, anointed Joshua with the ability to do so, yet if you read on, there were at least three occasions when God commanded Joshua to be strong and of good courage. Joshua had all the anointing he needed to lead the children to the Promised Land, yet God said to him that he would be faced with opposition. Joshua was not to look at those things, but to walk by faith and not by sight. In this world we will receive persecution, but Jesus gave us a command to be of good cheer because He has already overcome the world. In order to know your rights that are clearly spelled out in the Word of God, you must study them.

After God has identified specific work for you to do, you must study His Word continuously. Whether you preach from the pulpit or simply live it out in everyday life, you must prepare yourself by careful study of the Word to be approved by Him. Be assured that studying the Word of God is never a waste of time. Studying the Word of God is like sitting down and listening carefully to the words of a loving father. Allowing the Father to impart His words into you, where they sink down into your spirit, enables you to become a doer of the Word and not just a hearer.

"For if any be a hearer of the word, and not a doer, he is like unto a man beholding his natural face in a glass: for he beholdeth himself, and goest his way, and straightway forgetteth what manner of man he was" (James 1:23-24).

God knows the way, and when you allow Him to give you His words, it's preparation for the way. Again, refer to the words of God to Joshua. It was important for Joshua to know the importance of staying in God's Word day and night, meditating and pondering the Word in his mind over and over with the purpose of it becoming a way of life for him, so that he could observe to do all that was written.

God's promise in Joshua 1:8 was: "Then thou shalt make thy way prosperous, and then thou shalt have good success." Making your way prosperous means enjoying the accomplishments along the way. God has ordained for every man and woman to live lives of adventure along the way. Meditating on the Word of God begins a process that will help you reach goal after goal, time and time again. This is called moving from one level of glory to the next. It keeps life vibrant on the inside of you.

I started sitting under an anointed ministry in February of 1991, and by 1994, God had put many things in my heart. The teaching and learning process that was going on up until this time served as a Christian maturing phase, whereby my mind became renewed to the Word of God. In June 1994, the Holy Spirit directed me to start a weekly, one-hour Bible study in my home. I knew God could trust me to impart His words of wisdom through me because I had been prepared in many ways by the teaching that I was already receiving.

There were two gentlemen that I met who told me about their various backgrounds. One in particular had experienced similar heartaches and disappointments to my experience. My heartache came from a relationship with a sister friend of mine whom I had been fellowshipping with. I felt immeasurable love and care for her and the one thing I didn't want to do was to lose that relationship. She called me at work one evening and informed me that I was no longer going to be a part of her inner-court relationships. I knew that she was saying that we could no longer have the same closeness that we once shared. At that time, I felt isolated, hurt, and heartbroken. I literally cried because it seemed as though I was losing a pure friendship that I cherished.

I thank God for His loving embrace. He sent a saint my way that evening, another sister I met that night for the very first time. She stayed three or four hours past her normal work schedule to talk with me. (I found out later that she had never worked an extended day like that before.) Obviously, God connected us for the moment so that she could minister to my needs at that time. She could see the hurt that I experienced as she prayed for me and ministered the Word of God to me as a sister in Christ.

Brethren, God is sensitive to your every need! He heals the brokenhearted and binds up their wounds. I realized through that experience that God will not have us to reverence anything else in our lives as much or greater than Him. Yet, God, with His infinite wisdom, realized that the thing I needed most at that moment was an unconditional loving embrace and display of love. God knows what it takes to get our focus back on Him. God wants our relationship with Him to be the greatest relationship in our lives.

Now, because of my experiences, my heart went out to these two gentlemen whom I had met. I knew that if the three of us could get together and talk about the Word of God on a weekly, one-hour basis, it would take our minds off things that we were experiencing at the time. Also, it would allow us to build stronger relationships with God and each other.

They both agreed to the Bible study. But the first Saturday we scheduled to meet was called off, possibly because they had a change of mind. I remember feeling hurt and disappointed because no one wanted to come. Yet I was directed by the Holy Spirit to have the Bible study anyway. I hoped that someone would show up, even though it seemed that no one was going to come. I laid out my Bibles, notebooks, and outline for the Bible study.

As the hour approached for the Bible study to begin, I finally realized that no one was going to come. I didn't know what to do. But the Holy Spirit dropped a memory in my spirit of what my pastor had done years before. I invited the Holy Trinity and the angels of God to come. I remembered feeling a little awkward and strange at the beginning, but I invited them anyway. For the next two hours I taught as though the room was full of people. And even though I was the only person there in the natural, I felt the presence of God all around me. It's like God was saying, *It's okay, Robert, I'll come to your study.* I was emotionally overcome to the point of tears. God will never, ever let you down.

As I taught the Bible study alone in that room with the Holy Trinity and the angels for a solid two hours, revelation was poured into my spirit as fast as I could receive it. Many of the things the Holy Spirit gave me that day are contained in this book. Several days after the Bible study, I was riding on a bus, meditating on the things of God, when I realized that the Holy Spirit would not allow me to be despondent about not being able to share with those men what He had given to me. I heard the Holy Spirit whisper to my spirit that even though I was unable to share with them what He had given to me, one day I would be able to give it to other men in writing.

Several years have transpired since that day. There has been much revelation poured into my spirit since that experience. I'm reminded of what God said in **Isaiah 55:11: "So shall my word be that goeth forth out of my mouth: it shall not return unto me void, but it shall accomplish that which I please, and it shall prosper in the thing whereto I sent it." Jeremiah 1:12** reads: **"Then said the LORD unto me, Thou hast well seen: for I will hasten my word to perform it."** God is not unrighteous to forget the work and labor of love that we show toward His name, in that we minister to the saints. I was blessed to hear my pastor say that "time came out of God—God did not come out of time." So, before time was, God is. And we know that God is not going to subject Himself to, or be governed by, time. I am learning that when we go about our daily routines, praying daily to God and not allowing ourselves to be caught up in the time element, we will experience less or no frustration about the "due season process." After all, God said in **Galatians 6:9**: **"And let us not be weary in well doing: for in due season we shall reap, if we faint not."** To be not weary means to not have your strength or patience exhausted. Glory to God!

CHAPTER 7:

HOW TO GET PAST FRUSTRATION IN THE SECULAR WORKPLACE AND MAKE IT WORK

B eing in the corporate system, or the secular workplace, can at times present frustration and lack of interest. Christians in the secular workplace may experience frustration more often than non-Christians, because it's a system that's not necessarily designed for believers. Often you may find others of the world system appearing to prosper and getting ahead more than you, but it's important to always keep a good attitude toward your work and those around you. Always perform your work with excellence. If you do your work as unto God rather than man, you will not settle for mediocrity in your performance. Sure, you may see others cutting corners, or performing poorly in their duties, but it is never an excuse for you to do so. You may even see some people getting ahead through promotions and increase, but it's usually lost when gained unjustly. The Word of God has many things to say about wealth accumulated with a lack of integrity. **Proverbs 28:8** says: **"He that by usury and unjust gain increaseth his substance, he shall gather it for him that will pity the poor."**

God has a planned purpose for every level of our lives. When we display the love of God in our hearts, it emanates through us so that others see it in a manifested outward display. The particular workplace that you're in right now can be used to glorify God. Does that mean that you have to carry your Bible around and personally preach to everyone you see on the job? In most cases, I believe the answer is no, which doesn't necessarily mean that there won't be opportunities to share the Word in proper order. We can carry ourselves in such a manner that it arouses a natural curiosity in people. They want to learn about the joy that you display; they may want to know how it is you can remain poised when situations around you dictate differently. They may see something different about you, but they're not able to recognize or identify what it is. After careful observance, they'll come to you and inquire about it. That's when a platform has been set for you to glorify God by letting them know that the joy you have comes from the power of the Holy Spirit dwelling on the inside of you, and that they, too, can have it. **"Let your light so shine before men, that they may see your good works, and glorify your Father which is in heaven"** (Matthew 5:16).

We must always be in a position to allow the glory of God to show through us. We may have to be a "walking Bible." More often than not, the first contact a person has with God is through other people. Again, we have to be mindful that we do everything decently and in order on the job. We don't want to take time away from the employer doing things of a personal nature, even when we're ministering for God. God is a God of order. Even the Word tells us in **Matthew 22:21: "Render therefore unto Caesar the things which are Caesar's; and unto God the things that are God's."** And: **"Let all things be done decently and in order"** <u>(1 Corinthians 14:40).</u>

When we have an honest desire in our hearts to speak the Word of God to others to effect change in their lives, God will bring an opportunity our way. It will then bring glory to God.

Following Authority on the Job. When it comes to following authority on the job, there's a set standard or chain of command that is usually already established. The purpose for establishing a set order on the job is that it gives every individual a set assignment, and all can work together to achieve a specific goal or task. Each person in the process has an important role, no matter how menial it may appear. There is always a person at the top who sees the overall plan, and delegates authority to see that the plan is carried out. They are usually able to monitor each part in the process. That's why it is important for each person to play their part. Overseers are usually able to see when a function in the process is not being performed adequately, and will do what's necessary to correct the problem. That is why an individual must perform their particular task efficiently and effectively. It does not depend upon the difficulty or lack thereof of that task, because each plays a significant role in the outcome.

There is a principle at stake here. It is doing your best, or putting forth your best effort. Doing your best at one level prepares you to be elevated to the next level. It taps into a spiritual law: "**He that is faithful in that which is least is faithful also in much**" (Luke 16:10).

Although you may work in a secular environment, there is still opportunity for you to prosper through it. When a man or woman of God brings a high level of integrity to the workplace, the company benefits from it. There may not be an overnight breakthrough for you, but consistency in your efforts applied daily leads to success. No matter what it looks like from the start, a man of integrity moves forward. Some CEOs and other high-level officials in companies may have lacked integrity on the way up the corporate ladder, yet they seek to have loyal men and women around them. We can look at the life of Joseph in the Bible and see how he advanced in a system that was not necessarily designed for him. Because of his level of integrity as a man of God, he commanded the respect of his superiors.

"**And the LORD was with Joseph, and he was a prosperous man; and he was in the house of his master the Egyptian. And his master saw that the LORD was with him, and that the LORD made all that he did prosper in his hand. And Joseph found grace in his sight, and he served him: and he made him overseer over his house, and all that he had he put into his hand. And it came to pass from the time that he had made him overseer in his house, and over all that he had, that the LORD blessed the Egyptian's house for Joseph's sake; and the blessing of the LORD was upon** all that he had in the house, and in the field. And he left all that he had in Joseph's hand; and he knew not ought he had, save the bread which he did eat. And Joseph was a goodly person, and well favoured" (<u>Genesis 39:2-6</u>).

I believe that the time is *now*—when companies will seek out men and women of God to direct the affairs of their businesses. The most important ingredient lacking in many secular businesses is integrity when dealing with employees and customers. They need renewing in this area, and the field is wide open for people of God to show character and redirect the affairs of these major businesses.

So if you are currently employed in the secular workplace, do not despair. Let your consistent level of integrity sustain you even in the midst of great challenges and you will find that all of your efforts *will be rewarded*. In fact, the lessons you learn along the way can be used to teach others who may not be as well informed. Let the integrity of God rule in your heart! Remember the words of the psalmist:

"For promotion cometh neither from the east, nor from the west, nor from the south. But God is judge: he putteth down one, and setteth up another" (<u>Psalm 75:6-7</u>). Glory to God!

CHAPTER 8:

GET A VISION, HOLD ONTO IT

"And the LORD answered me, and said, Write the vision, and make it plain upon tables, that he may run that readeth it. For the vision is yet for an appointed time, but at the end it shall speak, and not lie: though it tarry, wait for it; because it will surely come, it will not tarry" (Habakkuk 2:2-3).

God gave me a vision for "Ambassadors for Christ Ministries" in the summer of 1996. How it came about, in my opinion, was miraculous. Several years ago, I worked a job Monday through Friday from 11:00 p.m. to 7:00 a.m. I usually took the subway each night, and I would read my Bible or books by various anointed men and women of God. Most of the time other passengers would sit down next to me. I've never liked just thrusting my beliefs on others (and I believe for good reason) because it may not necessarily be the time for them to receive. God, however, does know when their hearts are ready. I would always ask God that if He wanted me to minister His Word to the person, that He would first create an avenue for dialogue between me and that person. When He did, the anointing was there for me to minister, and for them to receive.

I followed this same pattern for several years, and one night in June 1996 while riding the subway to work, a gentleman got on at the mid-point station and sat next to me. I was reading a book by Lisa Osteen (although at the time I didn't know who the author was). A husband-and-wife team at my church were distributing pamphlets and mini books, and the book they gave to me was *Six Lies the Devil Uses to Destroy Marriages.*

So there I was, riding the subway and reading the book, when I noticed the gentleman sitting next to me was looking at the book. I asked God that if He wanted me to minister to this gentleman in some way, He would allow the gentleman to start the dialogue. Seconds after my petition to God, the gentleman looked over at me and asked, "Is that book you're reading by Lisa Osteen?" I had to look on the back of the book to see. Sure enough, it was. He mentioned that he had read some of her writing as well as some writings of her father, John Osteen. So, we started to exchange conversation back and forth, and he mentioned to me in a rather sad voice that he was going through the process of divorce, and that he and his wife were living apart. My heart swelled with compassion; I didn't know exactly what to say or do. I asked the Holy Spirit to direct my thoughts and speak through me the words this gentleman needed to hear. Immediately, the Holy Spirit directed me to speak these words to him: "Treat her with an unconditional love as your sister in Christ at this point." Then the Holy Spirit had me continue to minister to him that a display of love for his wife would stop any strife, envy, jealousy, hatred, or other ill-willed emotions that so often accompany divorces. I also told him that he would come to love her all over again in a different way if he would come to love her as a sister in Christ. Even if they were not going to get back together as husband and wife, they would allow peace and good-will in their hearts toward each other as they moved forward in their lives.

The Holy Spirit also told me to tell him to keep his wife in constant prayer because by continuously praying for her and being sensitive to the voice of God, he wouldn't allow evil thoughts to enter into his heart and he could quickly cast down foul imaginations. It's next to impossible to hate a person when you're continuously praying for them. It may often be a sacrifice, but it's one that is well worth the effort. It may not always be an emotional response, that is, we may not always feel like it, but we just have to make the decision to do so, and then do it.

After the Holy Spirit had me minister to him, He allowed me to pray with him. As we approached his station, I continued to pray. I realized that I wanted to give him my phone number so that in the event he wanted to, we could follow up with more prayer. I was searching through my briefcase to find pen and paper to write my phone number down. It looked like I wasn't going to get it to him before he had to exit the train, but a moment later the train completely stopped before it reached the platform, idled for two or three minutes, the doors remained closed, and there was no way for him to exit. I was overwhelmed by this occurrence and

I smiled, as it gave me time to write my phone number down and give it to him. God is in control of everything.

After the gentleman exited the train, I was still smiling and overwhelmed by God's presence and power. I thanked God for allowing everything to work out. Then I mentioned to God that if I had business cards, I would be better prepared in the event a similar situation occurred in the future. But then I began to think that I wasn't in a business that merited business cards and I didn't want to think of myself higher than I ought to. Immediately, God spoke up and said, *What if you think of yourself as I think of you? You are an ambassador.* I said in my heart, *That's right, God! I'm an ambassador—an ambassador for Christ!*

The very next day, God directed me to go and see about getting business cards printed. In the days that followed, I realized that God had a greater plan, much more than I could comprehend. God put Ambassadors for Christ Ministries in my heart and gave me a vision. In approximately one week's time, God gave me a ministry, a vision, and an assignment to go down to my home state to hold a fellowship and speak to the men of my city. God knew that I was wondering in my heart why. Why would He send me? All I could think about was how they would remember the old me, the person I was when I left several years earlier. Surely all they would be able to remember would be the days I spent living a life of sin. How could they or why would they receive anything from me? Yet in my heart, I knew God was telling me to go. It had nothing to do with how I felt internally. I realize now that when we concern ourselves about what people are going to say, think, or do, we're being totally selfish, especially when God is planning an itinerary for us. We must get past selfish motives like that in order for God to bring out the full anointing in us. Other lives are at stake.

So I decided to accept the assignment and go, in spite of my feelings of apprehension. There were several things that needed to be done before I could make the trip. First, God had me to register the ministry as *Ambassadors for Christ Ministries International*. I thought, "International"? Here I was, putting all my effort into just trying to set up a small conference at the little community center in my hometown. God let me know shortly after that even though my focus for the moment was to set the fellowship conference for my hometown, He did not want me to limit my thinking to one specific geographical region. After all, when He gave the vision, He commanded, "Go ye therefore, and teach all nations." So I knew it wasn't to be limited geographically. The process for bringing the first conference together began around the last week of June 1996.

The planning stages were all new to me; I had no prior experience in bringing a conference together. I called ahead and talked with the people of the city hall who were responsible for renting the community center, and they gave me a confirmation date of September 6, 1996. I paid the deposit and they were generous enough to work with me to pay the entire balance in a couple of installments before the conference date. I was very excited about what God was doing. I knew that once the date for the conference was locked in place, I had two months to plan. I began to realize how the entire planning process was being orchestrated by the Holy Spirit because each time I made an initial step, God enhanced it. He led me to the next step, which was to look up all the area churches. To my surprise, I came up with twenty-six area churches and pastors. God had me draft an anointed letter telling the churches what I was doing and invite them to the event. The next thing I needed was an anointed praise team, or at least a couple of anointed singers, to sing praises to God. I had an idea about who I wanted to contact, but God dropped the name of a childhood friend into my spirit to call. In addition to being a childhood friend and dear brother in Christ of mine, Brother Oliver Humbles (who I am proud to mention, has become a pastor since that time) had been an anointed musician who also taught instrumental music. I had no idea how talented he was as a vocalist. I phoned him at his home in Baton Rouge, Louisiana, and shared with him what I was doing and all that God had put on my heart to do. I explained to him that I had already reserved the community center for the men's conference, and I asked him if he knew of any praise teams that would be willing to come. His words were, "Brother, I have a praise team and would be more than willing to come." I felt a rush of excitement penetrate my entire body. It started to become more and more evident that my steps were indeed being ordered by the Lord.

The next step of the process was to get a well-known celebrity, who had become born again, to speak at the prayer breakfast the Saturday morning following the Friday night service where I would be speaking. I wanted to get someone whom all the men would recognize and would be willing to come see and hear. I remembered a professional basketball player who had spoken at my church. He shared his experiences with the men of my church and how he had been all over the world, had experienced various successes in the world, yet esteemed his new life in Christ as the best thing to have happened to him. He had such an anointed glow about him when he talked about Jesus. I thought he would be the ideal person to have at the meeting. I found out that his ministry was located in Arizona, so for the next four to five weeks I was in contact with his office to arrange for his services. He had an open date for that particular time, but we never reached a final arrangement. One of the main reasons I wanted to see him come was that I felt that some men would come for no other reason than to see a celebrity. That was okay with me, because regardless, my plan was for them to leave "born again."

I tried with all my effort, even up to the last minute of the last week before the conference to get the minister there, but my effort was not working. I realized in the last few days that it wasn't going to happen. I realized later that it wasn't what God wanted anyway. It just wasn't what God had in mind. I asked Brother Oliver Humbles to speak that Saturday morning instead, although I felt that it would be a new experience for him. He graciously accepted the challenge with a humble and willing spirit. I'm convinced more than ever of what Joyce Meyer has said: "God is not looking for our ability, but for our availability." How willing are *you* to make yourself available to be used by God?

I had studied the Word of God the entire time and prepared a message that I planned to deliver to the men that special night of September 6, 1996. Just before I took the podium to speak that night, Oliver ministered the anointed song, "He Is Able." After he finished the song, there was a spirit of quietness, settledness, and peace that entered our hearts. I knew that without a doubt it was a great move of the Holy Spirit. Just before I reached the pulpit to speak, the Holy Spirit changed everything that I had planned to speak on, everything I had studied from my text and notes. The Holy Spirit had me give my testimony instead and allowed me to become completely transparent. I told them where I'd been in life and how God had done a mighty work in me that allowed me to become a "new creation in Christ." Glory to God! When I finished speaking I had such a sense of fulfillment come over me, one that I had never before experienced in life. To think, there were times when I thought about abandoning the whole idea about going to my hometown to speak.

Even after having experienced God do so many great things to get the conference going, I wanted to call it off. There I was, sitting down at my kitchen table pondering my thoughts of indecision about whether I'd really go or not. I had pretty much changed my mind about going. I just didn't want to go, too concerned about what people would think.

I decided to open my Bible and read the Word of God for some comfort. I didn't know exactly what scriptures I wanted to read, but I just wanted to read. I quickly opened my Bible up, and it fell open to the book of Luke, the ninth chapter, and my eyes immediately focused on verse 62. Incidently, this is a verse of scripture that I hadn't recalled ever reading before. These are the words of Jesus in **Luke 9:62: "No man, having put his hand to the plough, and looking back, is fit for the kingdom of God…."** I sat there for a moment feeling overwhelmed, speechless, disloyal, and convicted in my spirit. How much plainer could God have been to me? After a few shed tears, I just simply said, "Yes, Lord, I'll go. Forgive me." I didn't question anything else about the mission from that point forward.

Part of my message to the entire Body of Christ (and not just to the men) is to pray for completion in the things we are doing for God. We must be aware that opposition comes, but it never has to overcome. We must understand that satan's mission is to *steal, kill, and destroy*, but we as Christians have been given power over the enemy and all his work, and nothing by any means shall harm us.

I believe that when your opposition is greatest, your breakthrough is even nearer. We must be reminded that satan is a spirit and he sees in the spirit the blessings God is sending to us. That's why the opposition may be stronger—because the blessing is closer. Satan's attack is to get your focus off the promises of God. When you allow the element of fear to enter in, you cannot clearly see the promises of God through the conditions and circumstances you find yourself in. That's why you must maintain clear focus.

I believe that we are at the beginning stages of a tremendous outpouring of blessings upon the entire Body of Christ. Focusing on God's promises puts you in a position to receive as long as you have great expectation. Glory to God!

"**Cast thy bread upon the waters: for thou shalt find it after many days**" (<u>Ecclesiastes 11:1</u>). We see many signs along the way in the path of life, many of which can be used later to glorify God. Again, let me refer to one of my boyhood experiences. One of the things I liked to do the most was going out on the ponds and lakes to fish. I found such peace and tranquility fishing. One of the things I noticed when I dropped bread into the water was that it would slowly float out into the center of the lake. When the conditions were right, the wind and waves of the water would ride the bread back toward the shoreline, a process that usually took days. I would often go back to the lake days later, and to my surprise, I'd see the bread lying at the shoreline. It was *always* magnified, expanded, or puffed up three to four times its original size. Being a young boy, I didn't understand that; it intrigued me and aroused my curiosity why the bread always expanded like that. Today, I know what the substance is in bread that causes it to expand when placed in water—yeast. We don't see yeast in bread, but it's there. A small measure of yeast is in most bread. *We may not see or recognize that faith (yeast) is in every man, but it's there.* "**God hath dealt to every man the measure of faith**" (**Romans 12:3**). You may not always see the expanded version of your vision right from the start, but when you put your faith to work, keep believing. Understand that the process of time and due season will come back with results magnified many times over, to the glory of God. Cast thy gift upon the anointing. It takes the water to make the yeast expand in the bread. That water is a purifier (anointing) on your vision to expand it to its fullest capacity. The wind blows the bread back to the shoreline. God will bring your vision to pass!

Jesus said in **John 3:8: "The wind bloweth where it listeth, and thou hearest the sound thereof, but canst not tell whence it cometh, and whither it goeth: so is every one that is born of the Spirit."** I call those gentle winds the "breath of God." We don't know exactly when the winds of change are going to blow into our lives, but we must be in a place of obedience with God, keeping our hands busy in the things of God and being flexible enough to ride the waves to God's destination for us. There is a substance in us called faith, which, like the yeast, causes us to expand when we cast it into the water (anointing). And when the anointing hits us, we're never the same again. Cast thy bread, and dedicate thy gift! Amen.

CHAPTER 9

WHY MEN OUGHT ALWAYS TO PRAY

There are several reasons why men ought always to pray.

1. Prayer gets our self-will out of the way.
2. Prayer puts us in a position to be directed by the Holy Spirit.
3. Prayer gives us confidence in who we are in Christ.
4. Prayer puts us on the road to our calling.
5. Prayer gives us strength to face the daily opposition brought on by the world.
6. Prayer equips us to be leaders of our households.
7. Prayer equips us to always be prepared to give a word.

"The Lord GOD hath given me the tongue of the learned, that I should know how to speak a word in season to him that is weary: he wakeneth morning by morning, he wakeneth mine ear to hear as the learned" (Isaiah 50:4). Jesus set the standard for praying. Although He was both human and divine, He recognized that without the Father, He could do nothing. He prayed continuously to the Father, and it was called a lifestyle of prayer. He continuously glorified the Father in heaven. In **John 8:28-29**, Jesus spoke these words: **"As my Father hath taught me, I speak these things. I do always those things that please him."**

Jesus knew that He could not trust in or rely on the things that He was experiencing in the flesh. **Matthew 26:36-42** reads: **"Sit ye here, while I go and pray yonder. And he took with him Peter and the two sons of Zebedee, and began to be sorrowful and very heavy. Then saith he unto them, 'My soul is exceeding sorrowful, even unto death: tarry ye here, and watch with me.' And he went a little farther, and fell on his face, and prayed, saying, 'O my Father, if it be possible, let this cup pass from me: nevertheless not as I will, but as thou wilt.' And he cometh unto the disciples, and findeth them asleep, and saith unto Peter, 'What, could ye not watch with me one hour? Watch and pray, that ye enter not into temptation: the spirit indeed is willing, but the flesh is weak.' He went away again the second time and prayed, saying, 'O my Father, if this cup may not pass away from me, except I drink it, thy will be done.'"**

Through these verses, it appears that Jesus was experiencing a powerful tug on His flesh, and He recognized the human element in Him. Yet He made a spiritual decision not to rely upon it, but give His will over to the Father in prayer. If Jesus had to rely upon prayer to the Father, how much more do you and I need the power, protection, and renewal of prayer to sustain us in our daily lives?

You may have good ideas or intentions, but in a spiritual sense, it's a willing spirit, housed in weak flesh. You cannot base your existence upon fleshy or carnal things. Jesus set the standard so that you would understand as a follower of Christ and not allow for any reliability on the flesh. Jesus is the standard setter.

In spite of Jesus' daily ministry of preaching and healing, He moved beyond the desires of the flesh and rose early each morning to pray. Paul tapped into the revelation of setting aside the flesh and carnal impulses as a way of guidance, and received the Spirit of Christ as the bond to liberty and freedom. In Romans 7:14-15, Paul wrote: "For we know that the law is spiritual: but I am carnal, sold under sin. For that which I do I allow not: for what I would, that do I not; but what I hate, that do I." Verse 18 states: "For I know that in me (that is, in my flesh) dwelleth no good thing: for to will is present with me; but how to perform that which is good I find not." And verses 22, 23, and 25 read: "For I delight in the law of God after the inward man: but I see another law in my members, warring against the law of my mind, and bringing me into captivity to the law of sin which is in my members. I thank God through Jesus Christ our Lord. So then with the mind I myself serve the law of God; but with the flesh the law of sin."

"There is therefore now no condemnation to them which are in Christ Jesus, who walk not after the flesh, but after the Spirit" (Romans 8:1).

Prayer Equips Us to Be Leaders. Again, Jesus is the standard setter. We must remember that Jesus was responsible not only for healing the sick and preaching daily, He had a group of disciples who depended on Him daily for directions. Luke 5:2-3 reads: "And saw two ships standing by the lake: but the fishermen were gone out of them, and were washing their nets. And he entered into one of the ships, which was Simon's, and prayed him that he would thrust out a little from the land. And he sat down, and taught the people out of the ship." The fishermen were gone out of the ship, and were washing their nets. They tried unsuccessfully in every way they knew to bring in a harvest, but to no avail. All their efforts had failed. The anointing had entered into the ship and put the entire situation in a different perspective. Glory! Now supernatural things could begin to happen. Jesus commanded Simon, "Thrust out a little from the land." He only had to step out a little from his familiar territory, just put out a little effort.

"Now when he had left speaking, he said unto Simon, 'Launch out into the deep, and let down your nets for a draught. And Simon answering said unto him, 'Master, we have toiled all the night, and have taken nothing: nevertheless at thy word I will let down the net" (Luke 5:4-5). Jesus told Simon that He was taking him out into the deep, a place where he had never been before, new territory, new surroundings. He would have to put his trust in Jesus. Jesus told him to let down the nets and put away his defenses, all of the old familiar ways of doing things, so that he could experience a draught like never before. Simon had no idea that he was about to witness an anointing that he had never known before. Jesus wanted Simon to know that He is able to do exceeding, abundantly above all that he could ask or think because that same power would one day be working in him. Glory to God!

Simon was saying that he had been a fisherman all his life with success. That particular night just wasn't a good night, because had it been, he would have found the fish based on his experience as a fisherman. Simon concluded that because Jesus said it, he would let down one of the nets. He had nothing to lose—rewashing one net was not as bad as washing all of the nets again. Luke 5:6-8 says: **"And when they had this done, they inclosed a great multitude of fishes: and their net brake. And they beckoned unto their partners, which were in the other ship, that they should come and help them. And they came, and filled both the ships, so that they began to sink. When Simon Peter saw it, he fell down at Jesus' knees, saying, Depart from me; for I am a sinful man, O Lord."** Simon was overwhelmed by the anointing of Jesus.

The blessings were greater than they were prepared to receive, although Jesus commanded them to get in position to receive it. **"The blessing of the LORD, it maketh rich, and he addeth no sorrow with it"** (Proverbs 10:22). (Sorrow only comes when we are disobedient or partially obedient,)

"For he was astonished, and all that were with him, at the draught of the fishes which they had taken: and so was also James, and John, the sons of Zebedee, which were partners with Simon. And Jesus said unto Simon, 'Fear not; from henceforth thou shalt catch men'" (Luke 5:9-10). Jesus knew they were astonished at the great harvest of fish, but He let them know that there would be an even greater harvest prepared for them as they labored for Him, and that they would have the anointing to do so.

"Then he saith unto his disciples, 'The harvest truly is plenteous, but the labourers are few; pray ye therefore the Lord of the harvest, that he will send forth labourers into his harvest'" (Matthew 9: 37-38). Jesus commanded in <u>Matthew 28:10</u>: "Be not afraid; go tell my brethren." And in verse 18 He said: "All power is given unto me in heaven and in earth."

Finally, Matthew 28:19-20 reads: "Go ye therefore, and teach all nations, baptizing them in the name of the Father, and of the Son, and of the Holy Ghost: teaching them to observe all things whatsoever I have commanded you: and lo, I am with you alway, even unto the end of the world. Amen." Glory to God!

PERSONAL PRAYER OF COMMITMENT

Father in heaven, I want to live my life committed to You through the Lordship of your Son, Jesus.

Since He laid down His life for me and rose again, I lay down my old life of sin this very moment and will live for You. I ask You to forgive me of all my sins and cleanse me from all unrighteousness.

At this very moment, I ask You, Lord Jesus, to come into my heart and be Lord and Savior of my life. Fill me with Your Holy Spirit.

I accept Your assignment for my life. My life now belongs to You. Help me, dear Lord, to walk in the integrity and character of Jesus.

Thank You, Father, for my new life starting right now, In Jesus' name.

Amen!

_____

Signature

_____

Date

ABOUT THE AUTHOR

Robert Daniels resides in Tulsa, Oklahoma, and is an active member of *Victory Christian Center,* founded by Pastors Billy Joe and Sharon Daugherty.

For the last two years, he has had the privilege to teach the Connect class "Barrier Breakers," whose motto is "Take your vision to new heights, overcome self-imposed limitations to realizing your dreams."

The purpose for this book is to teach men godly principles and inspire them to move into the plans and purposes of God for their lives.

Robert is a minister of God and is open for motivational speaking, church conferences, and men's conferences.

To contact the author, you may call or write:
Robert E. Daniels
P.O. Box 701294
Tulsa, OK 74170-1294
Telephone: 918-282-9841